AF228163

THE BIG 5: AFRICAN SAFARI ANIMALS
LION
A&D Xtreme
An imprint of Abdo Publishing
abdobooks.com
RUBY DANIELS

TAKE IT TO THE XTREME!

GET READY FOR AN EXTREME ADVENTURE!
THE PAGES OF THIS BOOK WILL TAKE YOU INTO
THE THRILLING WORLD OF ICONIC AFRICAN ANIMALS.
WHEN YOU HAVE FINISHED READING THIS BOOK, TAKE THE
XTREME CHALLENGE ON PAGE 45 ABOUT WHAT YOU'VE LEARNED!

ABDOBOOKS.COM

Published by Abdo Publishing, a division of ABDO, PO Box 398166, Minneapolis, Minnesota 55439.
Copyright © 2026 by Abdo Consulting Group, Inc. International copyrights reserved in all countries.
No part of this book may be reproduced in any form without written permission from the publisher.
A&D Xtreme™ is a trademark and logo of Abdo Publishing.
Printed in the United States of America, North Mankato, MN.
052025
092025

Design: Kelly Doudna, Mighty Media, Inc.
Production: Mighty Media, Inc.
Editor: Katherine Chu

Cover Photograph: JasonPrince/iStockphoto

Interior Photographs: Anna-Carina Nagel/Shutterstock, pp. 8-9; Betti Matteo/Shutterstock, pp. 42-43;
    Catchlight Lens/Shutterstock, pp. 30-31; Dagmara Ksandrova/Shutterstock, pp. 16-17; Dream Frame
    Photography/Shutterstock, pp. 6-7; Henk Bogaard/Shutterstock, pp. 18-19; IsNo/Shutterstock,
    pp. 14-15; JasonPrince/iStockphoto, p. 1; Jez Bennett/Shutterstock, pp. 20-21; John Lindsay-Smith/
    Shutterstock, pp. 28-29; Juergen_Wallstabe/Shutterstock, pp. 38-39; Kakuli/Shutterstock, pp. 32-33;
    Katiekk/Shutterstock, pp. 36-37; kongsak sumano/Shutterstock, pp. 22-23; Maggy Meyer/Shutterstock,
    pp. 34-35, 44; Michael Rads/Shutterstock, pp. 10-11; MP_Foto/Shutterstock, pp. 40-41; Silvia Truessel/
    Shutterstock, pp. 26-27; Simon Dannhauer/Shutterstock, pp. 24-25; Stu Porter/Shutterstock, pp. 12-13;
    Volodymyr Burdiak/Shutterstock, pp. 4-5

Design Elements: DGIM studio/Adobe Stock (distressed texture); Ografica/Adobe Stock (header
    background); Zebra Finch/Adobe Stock (header background)

LIBRARY OF CONGRESS CONTROL NUMBER: 2024948563
PUBLISHER'S CATALOGING-IN-PUBLICATION DATA
Names: Daniels, Ruby, author.
Title: Lion / by Ruby Daniels
Description: Minneapolis, Minnesota : Abdo Publishing, 2026 | Series: The big 5: African safari animals |
    Includes online resources and index.
Identifiers: ISBN 9781098296339 (lib. bdg.) | ISBN 9798384917762 (ebook)
Subjects: LCSH: Lion--Juvenile literature. | Big cats--Juvenile literature. | Big game animals--Africa--Juvenile
    literature. | Carnivorous animals--Juvenile literature. | Safaris--Juvenile literature.
Classification: DDC 591.96--dc23

CONTENTS

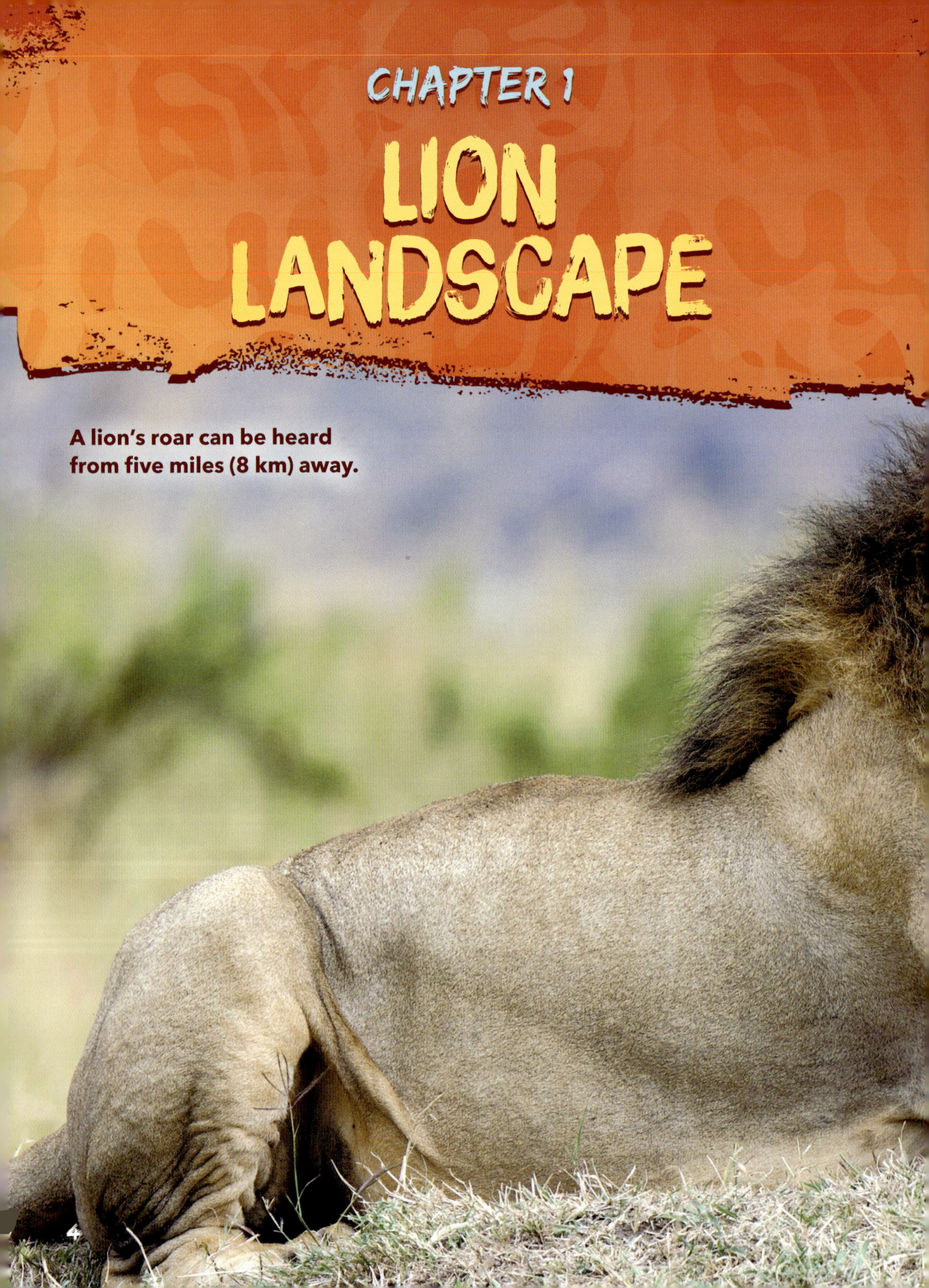

CHAPTER 1

LION LANDSCAPE

A lion's roar can be heard
from five miles (8 km) away.

You're on a safari in Kenya. Suddenly, you hear a sound like thunder. Your safari guide says it was a lion's roar! As you continue through the **savanna**, a group of big cats comes into view. One of them has a dark, furry mane. You've just spotted a pride of lions!

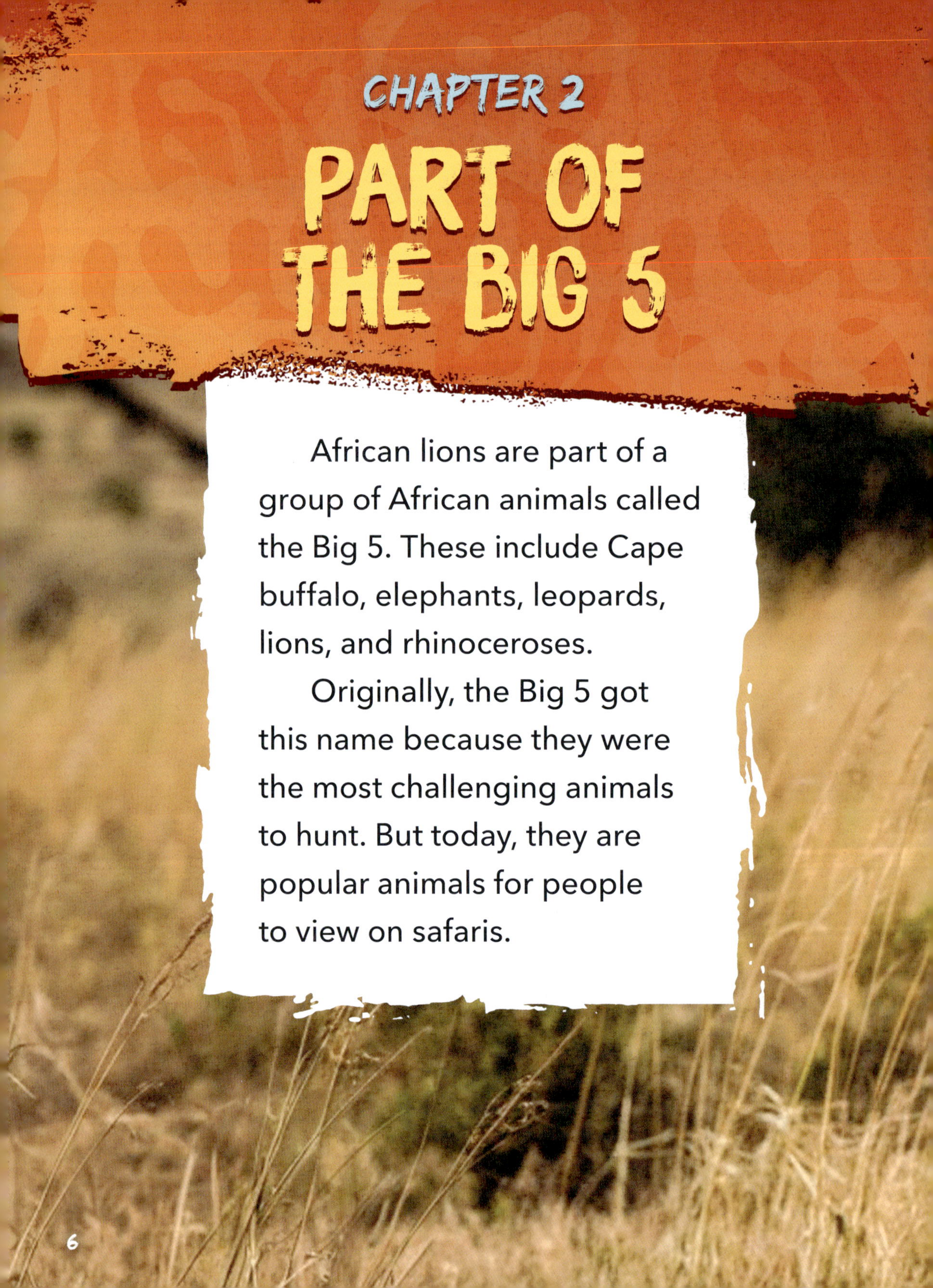

CHAPTER 2

PART OF THE BIG 5

African lions are part of a group of African animals called the Big 5. These include Cape buffalo, elephants, leopards, lions, and rhinoceroses.

Originally, the Big 5 got this name because they were the most challenging animals to hunt. But today, they are popular animals for people to view on safaris.

Simba means "lion" in Swahili.

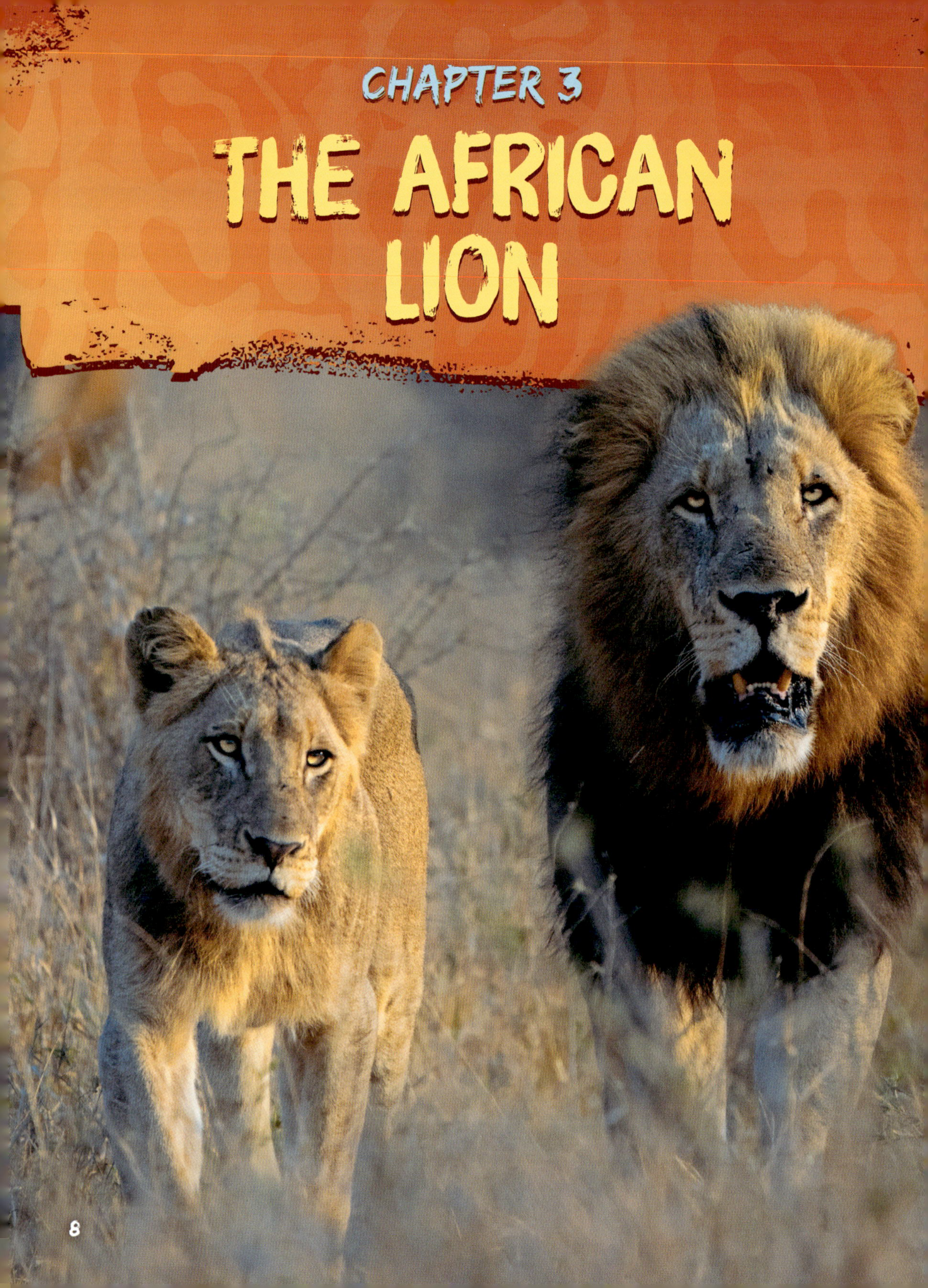

CHAPTER 3
THE AFRICAN LION

The African lion is the second-largest big cat. A male lion stands up to 4 feet (1.2 m) tall at the shoulder. It weighs up to 500 pounds (226.8 kg). It can be up to 10 feet (3m) long. That's as long as a standard basketball hoop is tall! Females are much smaller than males.

Lions are muscular cats with large heads. They are the only cats that have a mane. A mane is longer hair that surrounds the head and neck. Lion manes can be dark in color. Usually, only male lions have a mane. Manes help them scare other males and **impress** female lions.

Lions' manes can be
different colors and
shades of blond,
brown, and black.

XTREME FACT

Lions' whiskers grow from dark spots on their face. The spots create a pattern that is so unique, scientists use it to tell lions apart.

Lions are the only cats with a tuft of fur at the end of their tail. They use their tail for balance. Lions also use their tail to signal to other lions during hunts.

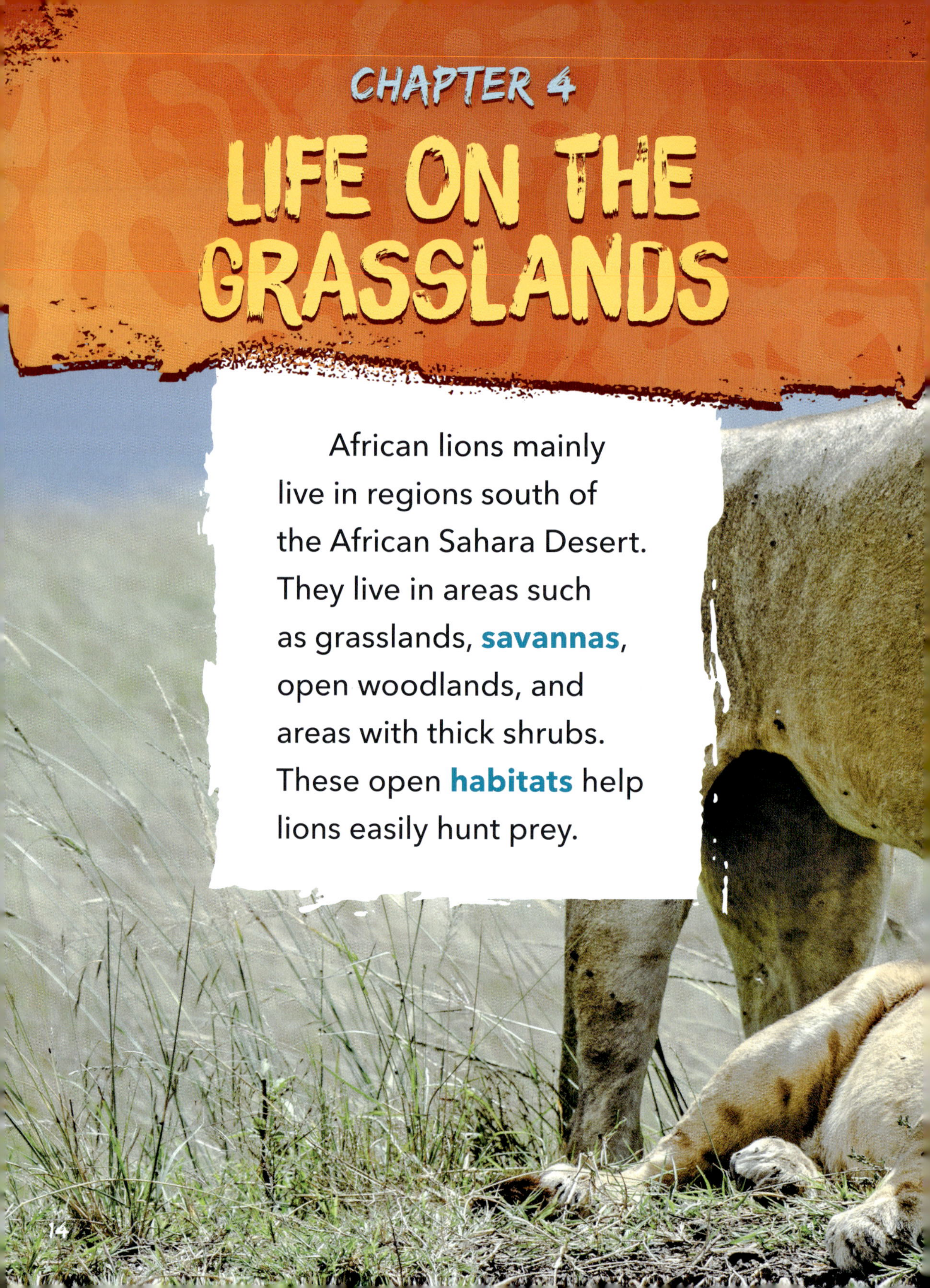

LIFE ON THE GRASSLANDS

African lions mainly live in regions south of the African Sahara Desert. They live in areas such as grasslands, **savannas**, open woodlands, and areas with thick shrubs. These open **habitats** help lions easily hunt prey.

A lion's lifespan is rarely
longer than 12 to 16 years
in the wild. They live much
longer in zoos.

Most big cats live alone. But lions usually live in groups called prides. There can be between 2 to 40 lions in a pride. Each pride is made up of females, cubs, and up to four males. The pride's females are usually related. They stay in the same pride throughout their entire lifetime.

Lion cubs are born with
spots. These slowly go
away as the cubs get older.

Male lions mate with multiple females in their pride. A female lion's **gestation** period is about three and a half months. They have one to four cubs per litter. The pride's females raise cubs as a group.

Lions are **carnivores**. They eat antelope, zebras, wildebeests, and more. Females do most of the hunting for their pride. Males claim and **defend** their pride's territory. They mark it with **urine** and roar loudly to warn other animals off.

A lion's prey is usually faster than the lion. So, lions must work as a team to hunt these animals.

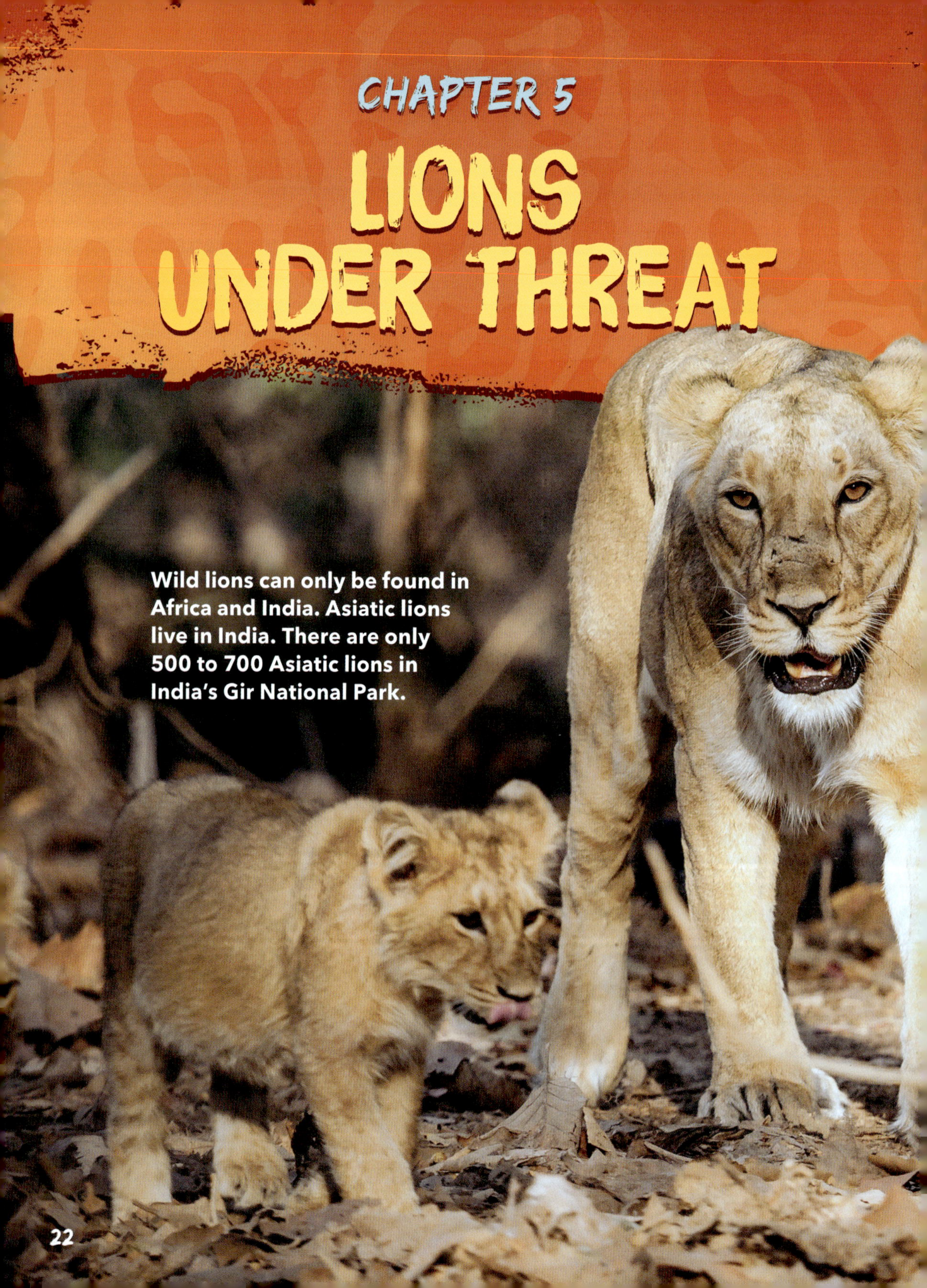
CHAPTER 5
LIONS
UNDER THREAT

Wild lions can only be found in
Africa and India. Asiatic lions
live in India. There are only
500 to 700 Asiatic lions in
India's Gir National Park.

Lions are vulnerable. This means the **species** is at high risk of becoming **extinct** in the wild. Lions have disappeared from 90 percent of the lands where they used to live. They continue to face many threats, mostly from humans. These include poaching, human-lion conflict, and **habitat** loss and fragmentation.

Poaching is a form of illegal hunting. People poach lions for their skin, claws, teeth, and bones. They sell these parts at illegal markets.

People also poach wild animals such as antelope for their meat. This is called **bushmeat** hunting. It reduces the number of prey animals lions can hunt. This means lions may not have enough to eat.

Problems also occur when humans and lions live near each other. For example, lions may eat ranchers' livestock. And ranchers may kill lions to prevent them from doing this. This is called human-lion conflict.

Droughts also lead to less prey and increased human-lion conflict. With less prey, hungry lions will starve or eat livestock.

Male lions roam long distances to mate with female lions. Habitat fragmentation limits their movement. This makes it harder for males to breed with different females.

28

Humans take over a lot of the land where lions live. This causes **habitat** loss and fragmentation. Habitat loss is when the size of an animal's habitat is reduced. A smaller habitat means less prey and more battles between lions for territory.

Habitat fragmentation is when an animal's habitat is broken up. This makes it hard for lions to mix with other prides. It also causes **inbreeding** and **genetic** issues.

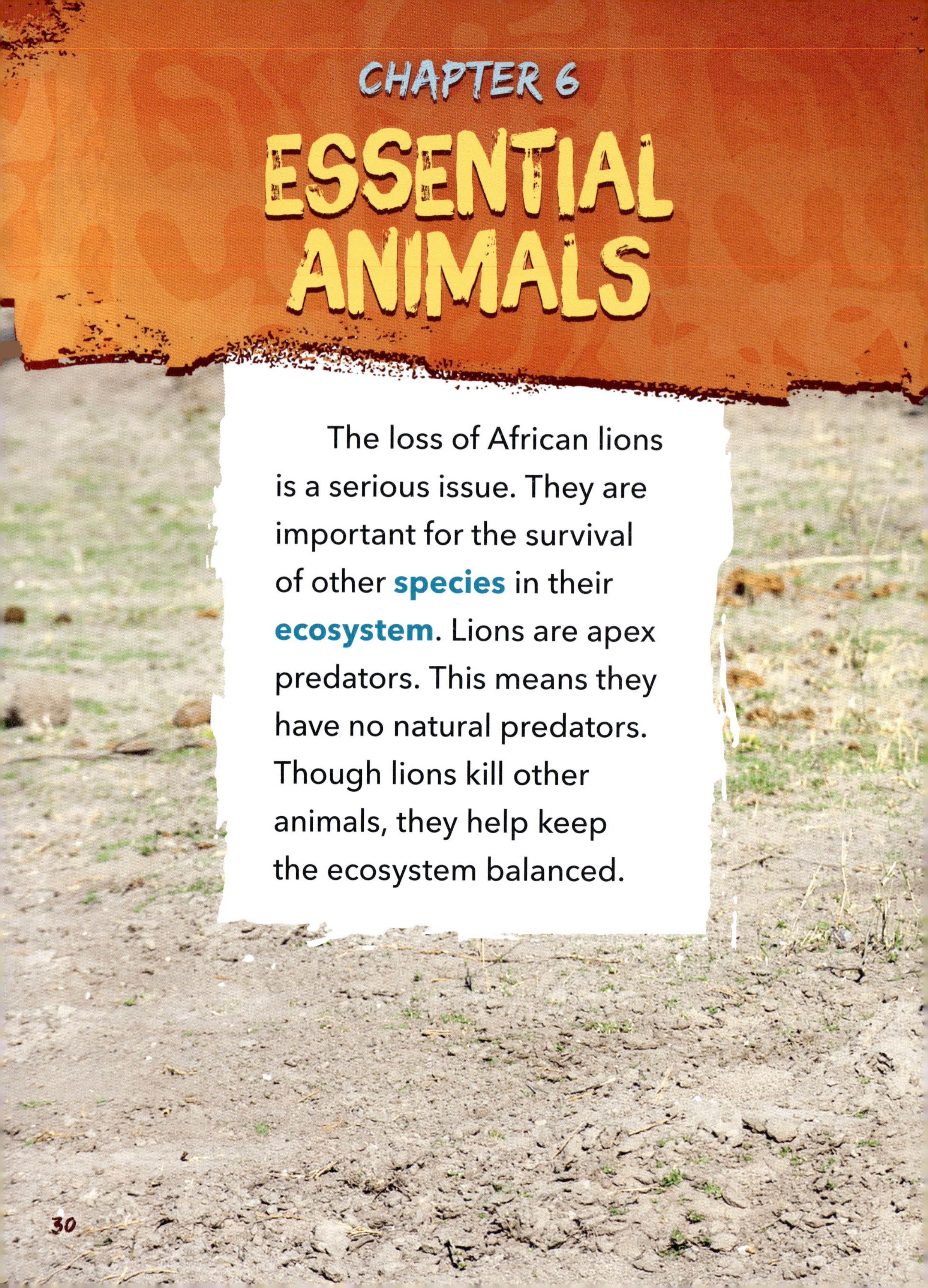

CHAPTER 6

ESSENTIAL ANIMALS

The loss of African lions is a serious issue. They are important for the survival of other **species** in their **ecosystem**. Lions are apex predators. This means they have no natural predators. Though lions kill other animals, they help keep the ecosystem balanced.

Lions need about 11 to 15 pounds (5 to 7 kg) of meat per day.

By killing their prey, lions control the populations of **herbivores**. Without lions, herbivores would become overpopulated. This means there wouldn't be enough plants for all the herbivores to eat.

With fewer **herbivores**, there is also a greater variety of plants. This helps smaller animals such as birds flourish.

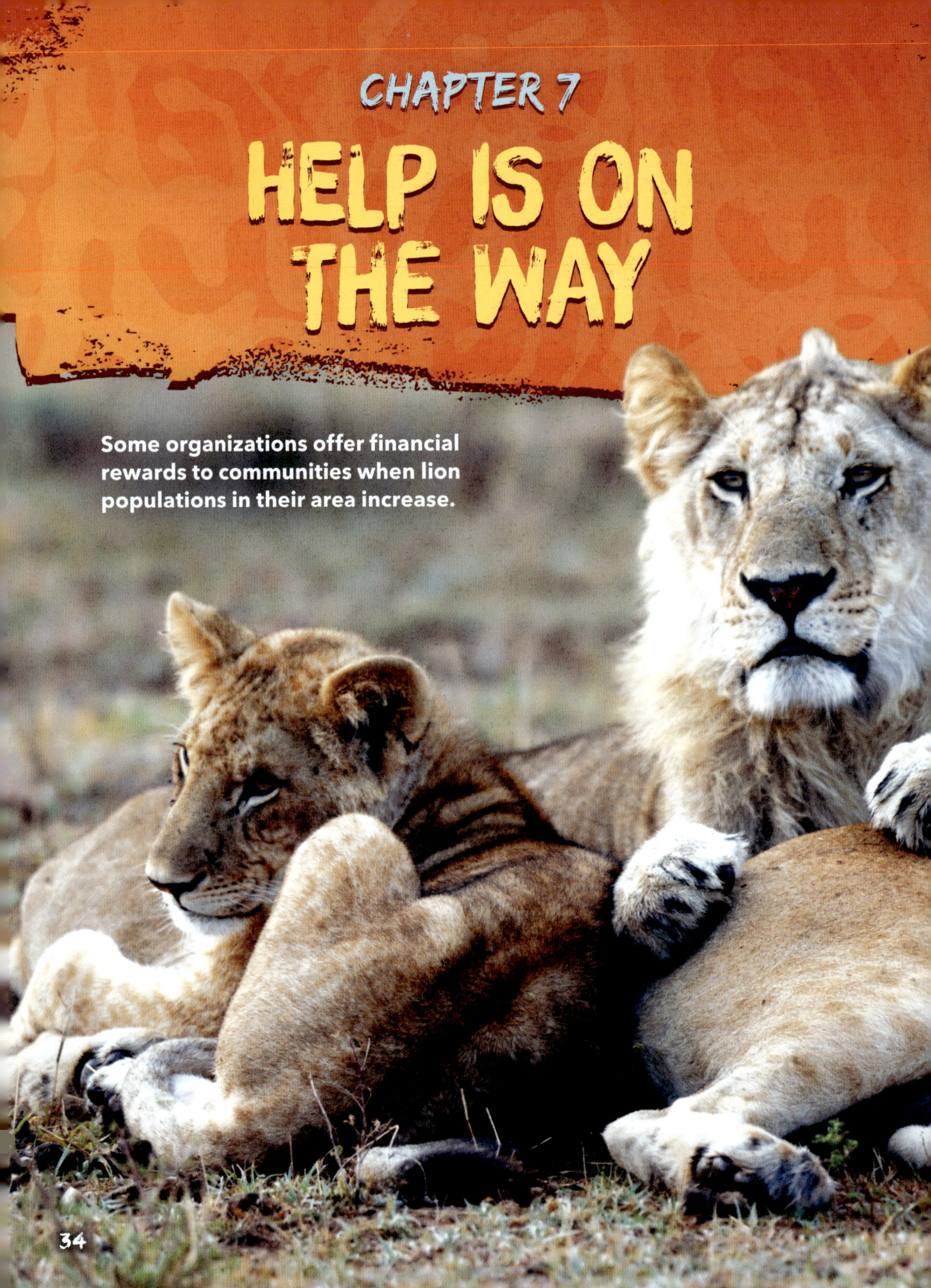

CHAPTER 7

HELP IS ON THE WAY

Some organizations offer financial rewards to communities when lion populations in their area increase.

Conservationists work hard to protect African lions. Organizations help **law enforcement** find and stop poachers. They also help people who rely on **bushmeat** for income find other jobs. The organizations also educate communities on the harm caused by poaching and train them to stop poachers.

Some organizations try to lessen human-lion conflict. Ranchers lose money when lions kill their livestock. The organizations raise money to pay ranchers when this happens so lions aren't killed in response. These organizations also help communities find ways to safely keep lions away from livestock.

Herders and ranchers in Africa rely on their livestock to feed their families and earn a living.

Many organizations try to prevent **habitat** loss and fragmentation. They **research** lions' habitats so they can learn what areas people should not build on.

Collars also help conservationists track the movement of lions. The collars tell them what areas lions use to travel. Conservationists can then protect those areas.

Other organizations manage national parks. These are safe places that protect animals from poaching. The organizations also **reintroduce** lions into parks where they had become **extinct**.

CHAPTER 8

FAN FAVORITES

African lions are popular animals to view on safaris. They are **unique** and beautiful animals. People on safari may see entertaining scenes like lions roaring or hunting. However, lions rest for much of the day. Visiting a park with many lions may increase the chances of seeing them in action.

Some lucky safari visitors might see lions fight. Lions sometimes fight playfully. They also fight when mating, for prey, over territory, and more.

Lions don't normally climb trees.
But the lions in Queen Elizabeth
National Park, Uganda, do!

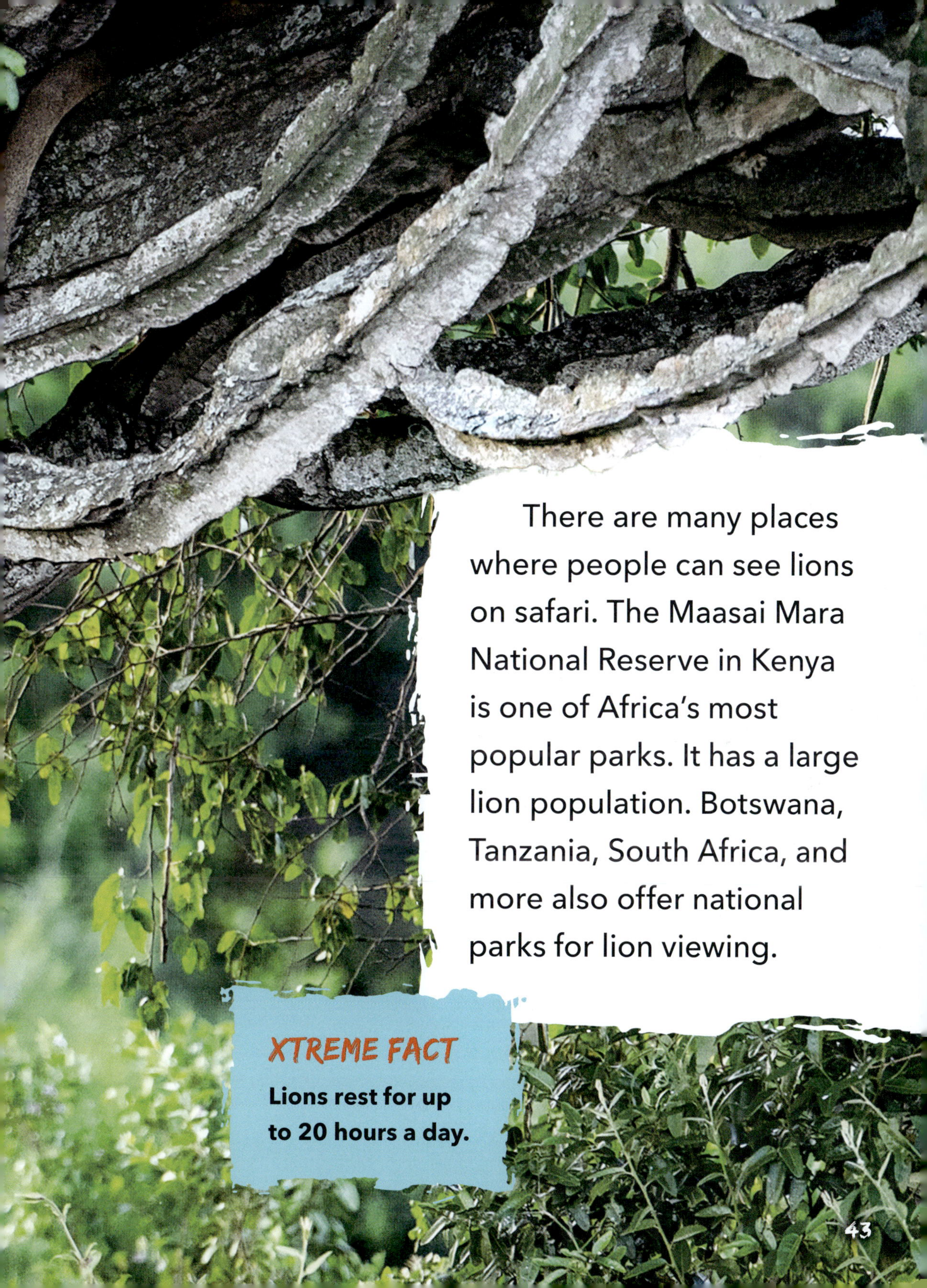

There are many places where people can see lions on safari. The Maasai Mara National Reserve in Kenya is one of Africa's most popular parks. It has a large lion population. Botswana, Tanzania, South Africa, and more also offer national parks for lion viewing.

XTREME FACT

Lions rest for up to 20 hours a day.

CHAPTER 9

MORE TO EXPLORE

African lions are magnificent animals. Their roars, manes, prides, and more make them **unique**. Though lions face many threats, **conservationists** work hard to preserve their **habitats** and protect them. Animal lovers can go on a wildlife safari and enjoy these majestic creatures in their natural habitats.

Many people believe lions are a symbol of courage and strength.

**TAKE THE QUIZ BELOW AND
PUT WHAT YOU'VE LEARNED TO THE TEST!**

1) What qualities make lions unique?

2) How do lions in a pride share responsibilities?

3) How does bushmeat hunting affect lions?

4) How are conservation organizations helping to reduce human-lion conflict?

5) Would you want to see lions on a safari? Why or why not?

GLOSSARY

bushmeat—meat that comes from hunting wild animals.

carnivore—an animal that eats meat.

conservation—the planned management of natural resources or animals to protect them from damage or destruction. People who do this are conservationists.

defend—to protect from harm or attack.

ecosystem—a community of organisms and their surroundings.

extinct—no longer existing.

genetic—of or relating to a branch of biology that deals with inherited features.

gestation—the carrying of a developing unborn baby in the uterus.

habitat—a place where a living thing is naturally found.

herbivore—an animal that eats only plants.

impress—to get someone's attention or interest.

inbreeding—when closely related people or animals have children, usually over generations.

law enforcement—a group of people who carry out laws, look into crimes, and make arrests.

reintroduce—to place or bring in something or someone again.

research—a study of something to learn new information.

savanna—a grassy plain with few or no trees.

species—a group of related living beings that can naturally produce offspring with each other.

unique—being the only one of its kind.

urine—waste material produced by the kidneys.

ONLINE RESOURCES

To learn more about African lions, please visit **abdobooklinks.com** or scan this QR code. These links are routinely monitored and updated to provide the most current information available.